WOOD CIRCLE

WOOD CIRCLE

John Wilkinson

The Last Books
Amsterdam and Sofia

CONTENTS

                  Download 9
Impromptu: Written on Water 10
                  Tabulate 11
                  Meniscus 12
Impromptu: Beyond Recall 13
                  Shed 14
                  Trial 15
Impromptu: Casts of Feeling 16
                  Hearing 17
                  Lay-by 18
                  Spool 19
                  Titrated 20
                  Burnt 21
Impromptu: Upper Lake Traps 22
                  Twister 23
                  Banquet 24
                  Studio 25
                  Pit 26
                  Lake 27
                  Argus 28
                  Rise 29
                  Stable 30
                  Temperature 31
Impromptu: The Done Thing 33
                  Volodia 34
                  Nameless 36

                  Al Noor 37
Impromptu: Lakefront Trail, March 38
                  Ripples 39
                  Interred 40
                  Concrete 41
                  Strand 42
Impromptu: Lake of Nemi 43
                  Rood 44
                  Ambassador 45
                  Store 46
                  Cruise 47
                  Beached 48
                  Crystal 49
Impromptu: The Decapitated Oak 50
                  Glinting 51
                  Harrow 52
                  Calais 53
                  Agni 54
Impromptu: For the Fallen 55
                  Thistledown 56
                  Pond-Life 57
                  Frontier 58
                  Stop-Out 59
                  Polyverse 60
Impromptu: In the Torch-Lit Wood 61
                  Upload 62

Torrid images circle in the wood.
Kingsley Amis

Lake acting up, up, uppity
Thylias Moss

DOWNLOAD

Unruffled by the breeze, water holds steady state.
      It must soon be shook, which mind is
shattering from black, white and brown,
into a leaf-fall flurry, green, red and gold:
      yes, in time, *understood*:
while holding form in the clear thought of water,
stalwartly supports its moorhens, its geese,
              its trumpeters
and passengers of one time continue to assemble
      to their slaughter. Flocked out of the sky.
Where in this world stands withstanding,
that will not ghost here and now in its imaginary:
      a notifying itch claims the good offices
of present sense, of attention, throws them right
into standstill, passport to
attachments shaped in metal, glass and plastic, up-
loaded firmware. Blinding speed
forces all receivers to dig in, their natures
arrive at their natures sheathed in attractive cases.

Beside a gravel path a mini-chalet tops out a little
stack of books, and at the shore canoes are laid up,
      paper shadows, plastic shadows
cast by forward-foragers long-past. 3D-printed
ducks amuse children;
much as an iron smooths a laundered bed-sheet
ducks take to calm. Music drifts equalised
from where people seem to be hosting an at-home
along the bank opposite.
      Stop for leaves to turn and fall,
      breeze to spring up,
evoke native ghosts right away to waver,
as receivers greet their evidence in coltered air
with stock faces drawn from repertoire, limited
to pleasure or vague guilt:
      how migrant birds forge onward! Time
to pack away, prepare for a great plummet
where leaves will fall that will have fallen already
green for the next wave of visitants.

IMPROMPTU: WRITTEN ON WATER

What is represented, is by dint of shadows/
      dint made to lick a surface/
            the skin of a dissimulation;
the more composed, less trustworthy.
Imagining to walk on water you leave footprints.

A dint is not a virtue
            (by virtue of...)
but an impression, as a lake's lustre even filmy
or lack-lustre;
never to put forth in lizard casts
      dints that the lake lacks, wind licks.
If anything birds' plummets were suspenseful.

Edicts ripple harmlessly where pretty children
gossip in their yards,
            swoop, swoop;
the skyline forbids dispersal,
wanting to contain dint shifty within its scope.
    A moving stasis.
               Rock, rock.

TABULATE

Beyond East Lake a fenced-off and trackless wood
bends and roars, climates warp in cataclysm
– save invisible trails
radiate like spider webs from a blasted central tree.
Receivers of what. No-one here dares bite.
        Perfection in reception, re-clocked
(see regulatory statement below).

Go pastoral you'll drop your thread, you'll lose it
        intermittently
betray your nature, transmit-&-receive functions
close down, smell of creosote, smell of cedar.
        Frames make sense of cloud. Where sense
shrugs off, skin hears the better
                clamouring, abstract animals –

but I am human, as if human had been
hollowed out, a mere cast, an after-shock, a crease
        printed by a howl which in rounds,
a lake's ripples radiate
        about a bare stripped trunk.
                Reorientate.
Taste is no more than the last hiss of that message.

From farthest reaches the wake pulls faint foam,
light gathering if hesitant, pines jostle;
        other bestial worlds throw
shade on their descendants, startle audibly, spring
forward to the throat. Go wrestle
        earlier forms,
copied in the clouds now superimposed on them.

MENISCUS

                    Days lengthening restore
fresh-featured woods,
deer white-scutted bound towards the lake
in hopes to drink,
         there they circle never moistening lips,
I mean pastures new,
I mean headless
plinth of quicksilver pasturage,
tumbling to placate where lies a horizontal,
laid for ant palaces
         a slight meniscus, hollow dip,
neck scoop.
      Not for long.
Light flees, life has fled, one scaled-up head
blimp
            domineers,
being-thus thus moulded myriad takes
from ANPR tracking
         shifts as cloud or starlings,
whose mind is construed so by a think-fold
sensor bank:
The model has become the mind.
And he that occupies the cloud thrust
sickle lightning into soil;
                  sore earth reared up,
creatures staggered.

The cloud's forming boundary is a garrotte
composing the idea of sky as it throttles it.

IMPROMPTU: BEYOND RECALL

I feel to edge my recall sharp against a rail
                blunted I recall,
why should I strop and strop against the same
circadian edge

        only to forfend what gleams and scoots
way off on the outfold,
        when eyes fix on the near
knot in stone I've been working myself towards.
            Deliberately a tree

leans from out its stand, pointing to a brown
frothy stream where a supermarket cart
        glyphs an edge zone in its resting place,
mesh gathers twigs, a stiffened chub,

might be discarded eyeballs, a monstrous roe
or clumps of white plastic anti-shock.
        Snow skitters out of the mind's eye's
fretting away in its own recognisance.

SHED

Raising tracks to retrench What was that
crawls from beneath. Left no tracks
        before him
Yes there was a take-up but they took on
Yes there was a set-to but they set out/
              going where.

Had followed fire-lines but whose eyes
stray from the beacon.
           How many vehicles then
pull off to the shoulder, check the trunk,
check under seats.
        Did you count these, swarm
of flies, clambering crickets,

did you count circling hours, in orbit set
by satellite, or by restless
pods of rock/
                pressed on again,
expanding frozen rails with fire
so passed across closed gaps.
            There was a
pulling-up, a halt.
            What fluttered from the pit,
tallying myriads?

The further vista
gouged out of the ground, flopped naked/
obviously exhausted.
In clay synthetic opals lodged.
          Yes they took on so.
      Lifting tracks like fire ladders.

TRIAL

Shame seduce in its many options, scuttle
        absence or bereft prairie,
who are they to criticise.
Absence being a thing not a state, solid
            contrary pricked out
as if stars, will join them as a salamander,
        rise up. Hold this for reserve.

Steps to take today, a drop-down menu,
        onionskin bow,
        ornament a long passed-over
him what is now signalling away,
oh that's your game, join the dots.
Name your hoped beneficiary
        shaping up in guise of this splotch

– soot bullseye –
        early build and wobbly yet a focus
for the funnel-shaped energy landscape
        tapped as was:
a focal point unsticks
rotating and suspended in tracery of fire,
        no point more than notional.

                You may step down,
acquitted on all counts.
You'll be identified as a plastic varietal
disgorged along an ocean trench, no
        right to remain –
        hauled back, thrust out casually
into a plastic flotsam patch
supporting itself outside territorial waters.

IMPROMPTU: CASTS OF FEELING

Here come to a stop at a presentiment.
                    The edge I work against, grind I welcome,
this grind would set back to work exhausted
          bodies laid out on the lakeside,
touchstones for a mottled subjectivity, that I am, good for me,
        flinched into moral being,

thus makes a double sacrifice. Cloud that figures out
sprays another bloody shower,
          gasping castaways for totems
propped in reverential and evasive display. From here on in

the circle stays unbroken in its own eyes (eye roll),
          strops against a guilty conscience, feels sharp
          inside its frame, clenched against vagueness.
Outlandish activity glissades.
               I know what waits on the horizon, enough, so
stop before spangled waters and work away.

HEARING

The fiction of their voices the repining floor affirms.
Access to raw materials brokers a place.
The fictive is not the false.
                        The catch on a gate –
will fiction leant into by an iron stock then swing
          stamp of the real
                  deaf, inert on one aspect,
boards at his periphery to their hinges wake up –
for instance Abdullah Dilsouz, 15 years old,
run down by a refrigerated truck in Calais,
en route from Afghanistan to England, so close.

Here the hum of bulk transport has been banked,
mud glistens cut above the European perspective.
What 'deaf' means is not lost hearing,
but attitude to the must-go-unheard, swing
             to a machined socket. How
                     do you plead. It's true,
it's true. Even if afterwards I imagined it.
The gate across the way the deserted path it's near.

          How refuse a channel for priority boarding,
striding pre-approved and cocky?
               Sing along with what shows up,
an ice-cream van whose tune you default to,
      fault into. Listen to its catch,
that means catching on. *Don't.*
Just imagine his life. In the inexhaustible reserves
buried in our futures. Underfoot titans roar.
Shortly let rip.
Overhead the ministers of justice look elsewhere.

LAY-BY

       This voice, scrim of fabrication,
truth-effects that waltz and glow – poptones
embellish what they crop, said shrubs lure
foe to factitious kneeling at false dawn, overlap
        ridges might recall
                traipse day of ploughing,
traipse day across a trackless sky, spotter planes
drag day apart.

Freshets, water bottles, sopping soil vocal plays
Reach for the Sky in series:
        a ranked anthology of skies
has massed above a truck-stop gap. Struck
        rock overflows, tense the broad
river's muscle
under shrugs of sportive affable cloud –
don't look up else your skull scoops open-cast,
        Gods basically malevolent:

They spray your eyes when you are asleep.
It's very stressful living in these forests, cold
        fanned out still in veins,
                earth's brutal contract. We were
here long before but turquoise and aquamarine
visible in ridges we marched

        directed where to set our face,
celestial shadows gurn across the sectored sky.

SPOOL

Ringtone parroting its scales of endangerment, how
fiction be rolled out that will not shrivel
food-wrap but the floor undergird. Heartless
corridor, future cars thud against bleached boards.

Data miners flutter over banks, his panting bowels,
rolls of pink packets pierced with disposables,
Copper-64 for tracer in his marked blood, can
        them or us
                sensory carapace
violate him now? He had to walk himself back fast

granular, into the trench.
                Life support
you call it, rough struts, overhead is bulging
                              bagged hundred-
weights rise, skin and bone organise,
       giant spools unwind.
The wells are stained and silence striated,
                                    the road
has been resurfaced and you will not throw yourself
from the car. *Call from wireless caller. Ignore.*
You never will because you gleam like a staple
grips a chicane, splaying on the level in components.

TITRATED

       Make a stand on asphalt, pivot
white trunk, then uprooted lights flicker on
on gantries round the circle, pit's bounden spring
regulates the soil's adventive here-we-go
cicadas and intense rustle. Did that go well.
                Elaborated fiction,
temper flames' intensity, lower to compelled
flux, hardening as epoxy coats a sheet of oxygen.
Breathe it. Flint spark. Pine-needles. Arak.
Blow against the many faces, hard blow it was
      at the brazier, rubber bullets
Then a car jumped forward.

       Hounds are circling mad to shake
a blood-compacted cone constraining this gamut,
slow melt drips measured through its nozzle,
     soaks the forest floor thatch,
stiffens as a glossy apron:
                    the optic, the dispenser
stays authoritative, cannot be ousted,
turns unstoppably,
as a new-build foundation distorts the plough,
                      cooled cement
enraged gulls explore and shit over.

       Over here a hopper
gets constructed once trees are felled,
              here theoretical overview
bonds a sheet of teeming ground cover,
                         brick kiln
sinters minerals to a glaze
highlighting a charred haunch, diviners' bones.
Pockets hold vestiges of an earlier people,
     gaseous that stir and will reinfect.

BURNT

                 In those circles it was thought
a voice in the stands to commandeer, fight follow
down by the fire pit, faithful to script,
wrestlers stripped to their altogether, circle. Tush!
Not one hot dog. Not one glass of wine.
There was no such thing as a thing. That
                 deserves to be stressed.

      Return us to our senses,
thus, thus, hobnailed boots, kick senses back
from the circumference they have migrated into:
the wrack line, the running cracks on monitors
re-wound on their spool to now misbeget.
                 Scale the iridescent fresh cut.

The heart is denny and hollow.
Forasmuch a burr drill incises scrolls over its lid,
lid alive with natural history videos,
the elaborate fades into the tracks of leopards,
melting tundra. What was a thing afflicts.
                 Draw back, chilled or burnt,

                 the threads of destiny entangle,
hot wax drips on them and cools to affirm
simply where we are, each one their personal seal.
Across the slant wall of the velodrome, gamers
practice flip tricks, but on its central dais
                 a pile of entrails steams.

IMPROMPTU: UPPER LAKE TRAPS

Self-blame make ready to indulge its moral drama,
grateful to be rehearsed.
      A stack of beaver pelts
devoured by rats and distant traders,
a sudden drop in the price of crude –
            there was a failure of sentiment,
abstract conception of borders
      woven together tout suite,
went to overlay a more physical sense of Where,

where to belong entails deference to local ways,
strap on knee-pads,
      prayer being wet and voltaic:
short of belonging, co-existence
became more viable on planes exquisitely aligned,
            metaphysical traders

and their holy spirits learnt to hover above pins
holding flat the landscape,
      while those unhoused the villagers invite
to shuffle close to fire pits
inhabit one and the same place.
Rats then bite holes through its pretty fabric;
            pins designate
server banks that process
      biometric data, while stray agents
of metaphysics are grabbed and strapped to trees,
            flayed and beheaded.

TWISTER

Shield to outward face if forced against the wall,
calm at the storm's eye although metal chasing
writhes where waterspout, tornado
broaden in their spirals an hourglass lacking base,
    collage shield
where sand its systems volunteers which dissolve
to recompose – are local storms to be tracked,
flatten crops in spirals as though tremors
of high finance spark off an atmospheric frisson,
a fire infolding itself
    a wrap I'd call it,
        flare from Circe's maw.

Would this atmosphere extend your reach?
Does its turbulence sort with your declared taste?
What had seemed profligate drags its single point
through houses, high-speed whirring router
wrenching tiles and sidings
    splat against the wall-like horizon,
blocking first responders.
A tree whips its own trunk and contorts frenziedly,
and in adjacent storm the eye is the first circle
    Why say that,
        first circle is an anus
    dumps
ocular nightmare, festoons of scooped eyeballs.
    His car wrapped round a tree-trunk.
Did you want publicity, flashlights then in flash
photography, shit smeared on a wall, dirty
    protest, night
pyre inverted in the rocking wood,
burns metal, burns a brocade with sparked stars.

BANQUET

A face into its flesh ghosts on CCTV pear-shaped.
Trawled across the clamshell industries that sway
burnt-off plumes, jet deep-water plumes,
insignia of clamshell shielding violet shadows
of the sun's fist stopped down to blackest aspect,
looms.
         Beautiful as skim by rote,
                supernal like a freeway
banners hoist hieratics, solar panels, soda drinks,
Kunbey was from Chah village in Ngaba County,
enrolled at Kirti Monastery at a young age,
husk of get started cancel drapes on prayer flags,
scripts will have been pressed a spongiform
shameful struggle to put two and two together
         launched on a lagoon
              high table, theory
lackey to provincial leader or propaganda chief,
discovers rare earth deposits, states
events to be self-starting, sheds raise themselves,
laid on the horizon gap-toothed in chemical froth.

Points perforate, they lace the page,
attention drains, it's like a sieve. Tree language
says that is no downpour but the poplars' surging
above the medical research centre.

    I am nowhere and leaving
    You young people gathered here at the brink.

STUDIO

Even without airy stir, oak leaves clatter
        down denuded stalks,
dive onto dust sheets of guilt, prick and twirl,
sheets draping studio assets,
        to end up
counting for what on blood-soaked mattresses.
        Penny twists of paper flare behind
gartered skirting boards.
I reported this. I was my prosecutor.

Blush on maiden easel, charcoal twigs, rivets,
turbine blades:
        Multiplicity
through the springback soil bristles,
        mulch warms larvae.
Please to read prospectus, its pink polypus,
        without shame.

Among the culpable who stays impenitent?
        Crowded by root forms,
first growth a wooden floor claims,
scoured for sake of the people, the clean slate
        surfaces, stains expunged...
How many? How many? Paste wings
flutter through attempts
        to take them down. Still they live.

Singular spark, singular flame, it too thrives.

PIT

What was a fire pit, leaves the hole of soot
      charred stumps encircle.
          Thin out the brush. Their pure Nordic
            gaunt, silver-birch –
pert, decorative birds fill their branches
amid twinkling stars and snowflakes.
      Where did previous species
fly and scurry to,
where will new arrivals find a habitat
in the tinsel and chilly span of rectitude?

A line has been drawn.
      The hole of soot pouts with trinkets,
          folk art. Further down,
more singular abrupting,
whirl of a ghost dance in flames dying back,
a statute from the past century
anchoring its hasp, a wire span
      stretches out, reaches up.
What had been a rim of fire now eclipsed,
      slippery, perilous soot,

the one-time wellhead is a churning stoma
      dented canteens strew round,
collapsed canvas hoses.
      Cruel, despoiling firefighters
call this a day, each
hero has to down his glass and go. Many
trample, gadarene,
      when new arrivals
shedding tears get ripped from their teats,
to lie exposed in the acid shower of stars.

LAKE

Forgo its Appalachian song,
           casts of worms, disavow them –
the nitrogen of freeways will like bindweed
squirm after dawn,
soon as apartments have been checked out of,
        passed over by morning sun.

Autotuned and processed song at night whines
against wire boundary fences and the invisible
limits to domestic dogs.
      There are deals to conclude
upon earth, by picture windows propped

lines to ward off leaf-blowing
squads of yard workers,
        pick-ups turn over, their flashers going.
Can I circle back to you on this? Keep this
to browse

                transparent moss.
It is the writing of the firebreak that blackens,
        blackening to nourish seared earth.
Each creature is dying in our time, not its
species time but our time:
      Pull yourself together.
      Pull into the turning circle.

ARGUS

Was it his attaché or bodyguard, did it patrol,
forced through the channel like a necklace of
eyes looped outside his cave pitches downhill:

Training ardour on a belching stove he'd hug
behind a portal, protected, let others struggle,
       sockets failed in series,
               their fiery trail regenerate –
*But then, you're an infamous liar and if truth
meant anything your ship would still be trapped
in pack-ice – as it is you wallow among pigs,
with running dogs and chickens and roosters:*

He'd bilked a suit of cups slapping into slops,
braced autonomous in carbon-thick, scurf air:
for on the hour fingers detached would write
soot stalling down the plaister of a slate wall/
       from its volley blow back
           smutch he'd left
epitaphs. What stencilled letters blistered off?
Swells of insect noise thickening stale air,
fine graphite dust the headwind enshrouds:
fingers work on slate, panoptic its head count.

Mass lowing hymns the sun as it resumes its
scratching out: must be those animals
that wallow untallied in the pitches of ocean.

RISE

First water for such pioneers as stretch the bow,
in fellow-feeling gain refuge on higher ground,
its feeling lint might fail as aggregate in soft
cement crystallises, drying on its rods cracks up,
      trapped birds in vesicles,
            cars above deck hunched –
as would this asphalt lake absorb the pickup
parked overnight, who's got hold of its remote,
digesting carbon amid corpuscles, the gaseous
last gasp of a concrete boot, plunging in slow:
      Even so lint as cotton fuse
          Once more with feeling,
sunk beyond recovery but influential, cranes
nodded cables ferrying pallets over sticky surge.

A second wave was more powerful, as velvet
lines a frame stuck solid, light lines grey stacks,
in fading crowds the copse with headless if
spruced-up congregants. Call for a last swing
      against dying light perks
          laurel wreaths or bays
encircle frowning brows as they greet the dusk,
drawing lines between heart-breaking loss and
social decadence in the abstract, re-oiling wood
stocks but waving rifles in the air untargeted.
      Emotional pageant,
          box girder crane at quay-
side grabs at a crate. Bedstraw will be ignited
by stray arrows, cotton burst in buds of flame.

STABLE

Drive past a stable block sealed by a ditch,
cower in a smoking vault crossed by lines of fire,
    heart of straw aflame:
lines had been snagged,
       lines snagged to loop
spool off days and nights, will the vault crater
above the human sphere, time spit time in gobs.

This line must never be stepped across. Or line
be treated lightly, a line lays claim to one
thought to be present.
    Maybe it was the bench,
but a bench would seem too obdurate. Or else
up to you – but choosing ends in choice
secured to a place that declines:

drive back past the stable, its triple horsefly-
valve rises and then sinks at the initialised
    gateway of both access and overflow,
    lines tugged tighter.
There was a stomping, there were ceiling tiles.
Orgasms followed choking. Pleasure
to be taken from a line screws a collar tight.

Ditchwater spouts into the sky, the polder arches.

TEMPERATURE

Towards what would such selves draw and gasp
apparently, as though the curse of substance
had been dreamt through and let go –
  choke on flaking plaster, dwell
on heirloom merits, claw feet, costume of a still-
workable identity that blows eggs
  false as blood and feathers fly
across the human space, no pressure felt,
strewn about a needle-padded floor –
were they sensors or rudimentary organs redden
in the wake of Who's responsible for my tray?
  Inside, high pressure, a new low without,
prickles at its stress points everywhere, clogged

effluvia, so gas valves stud the universal heap,
a million vents and throat chorale work in outcry.
Kludges they might be,
  yet here perch all with love
as though one's cupped, vacuum-drawn circle
blew its closure straining to get pierced and now
just might open voluntarily.
    Insect valves settle, functionally
equivalent to portals into cold machines,
deliberating hiss, sectional prostheses to thought,
  shells multiplied in hapless thuds;

and yet this thud of earth, this hollow thud, thud
breaking in each breast against the circle,
  chokes, with its first order audible
before the shovel-full strikes the casket,
slackening the ligament between dirt and body
  – temperature has flatlined, says the readout –:
then life's availing, its breath-labour,
    moving through gristled air's
invasion and retreat, assents to the final compact,
capped by stone and by pine needles' gentle fall.

Outside selves walk across Central Park or down
  Thames Path,
towards any cocktail bar or café which might do,
  this is our field, this our rickety fold
of shared time;

and suffering dissolves in a mild, ironical smile
behind winking lights that indicate a body's less-
than-final state
      stayed and prepared for removal.
We shall remove, we all, we shall remove more
than anything accompany the senses
      weaving through dusk, let them out
of being confined in what's no longer measurable.

IMPROMPTU: THE DONE THING

Nothing here fits, nor should it
   be let them be
shadowed by the stone-cold
certainties taking back their words,

leaving the unnamed no more
   aspired as lumps
on the shadow strand. A renewal
guide tells you how to capture

people walking in the street
   but remain silent,
it is enough to incline slightly,
prise yourself away, any swarf left

sparkles. Stones do not speak
   but the setting,
its sharp dust is speaking volumes.
People look to their shadows,

draw to a standstill. Only waste
   light distinguishes
actions from their fit ends,
fringes where their outward going

toils back silent and unsettled.

VOLODIA

Who would hear were hearing a pith voice sheathed
        by the act of hearing?
What did he hold in reserve, with transmission
shrouded as though hearing's echo?
                      It is his inside
his singing hood his solitary his without feign swoops
about the ears.

Who would hear the dirt he will within his hood grind,
        would hear the harp a bough dangles
swept and struck,
threading through what's trafficked as his inside gen,
        genuine feeling –

        or spoken in the marrow out of hymnody
him whose likenesses were ghosting from his hood,
each more real than real, his starveling illusions flit –
                likenesses
not to be released even two years after dying
due to TB and his harsh repeated beatings, his name
effaced

                       _ _ _ _ _ _ _   _ _ _ _ _

      soaked mattresses

              belongings dumped after work –

not to be released in paperwork.

2

Image not to be retained on file, name to be revoked,
                          it has to be his blood
sings aloft, spiralling on thermal high alert, fit falcon
        killing with a look.
        My genuine likeness has the dirt.
My likeness swoops and cracks and jabs at bones
the mountain slope is littered with.

              Sky tumbled bones.

But he bore no likeness being stopped and searched,
        being naked as the day
he had been registered, he had been born,
        naked as the pith
beaten out to parchment where a death warrant
would be drawn up in duplicate and stamped,
        word-for-
word put to rights, carbon-sheathed:
                Volodia, Volodia, I hear you, do I.

3

She said I have your back. You know
        I'm your blood but I have your back. This dress
has many pockets. An apron of small instruments
        honouring your loved ones. I conceive
your dress as dirndl, and it flaps along the untrodden
        path towards the axis. As if a path
                could be untrodden.

Ocarina, finger cymbals, jew's harp, these stick out
        of the back they had been lodged in.
All the books sag. My back
        had been pecked by birds, my eyes were
saturated, there could be no travel, no divergence,
        no temperature gradient, no measurable scale,
                no skin, homeostatic.

Volodia, you will have died another death if two-by-two
swap words, swap looks, swap touches,
        high-pitched hash leaks from a leather hood –
                some vestige I seize,
claim for my interior voice, this skin of sound, this
        mantle I wear and hear and duplicate,
                turned out in my effrontery.

NAMELESS

What detains breeze amongst Karelian birches, hangs
unpicked in packets, fingered apart into its gusts,
       hangs much as leaves whose smudge and blur
arrest disturbance?
           As are too many names
to pass by word of mouth, and trees' collective
sigh catches no ear, for it is uninterrupted,
       and where a distant camera keeps a fixed view,
affectless,
               in catechising solitude
one leaf skitters. That's the one. Nameless.

Metaphors have been nailed down, sun has to glare:
         gash in one white bough exposed
to careless light,
no resin bleeds from nakedness, from obduracy,
nor does bark discolour.
       About the stricken lake
instruments await what once might have been tracked,
birds no more called on to migrate
                     Memory foam
holds a disregarded shape
       Names stay unspoken.

Could the local agent spare a moment's thought?
who apathetically reviews and records, his attention
            sighs scrolling down,
unspooling sky to stretch like blue plastic sheeting
wrinkle-free.
       Air's musculature
tightens at his temples but the impulse
                its correct way goes
from sender to receiver, no noise, no message.
The mummified corpses managed quite well in the water,
     floating not sinking.
Not yet tagged.

AL NOOR

They all look forward but their eyes still dilated
bump against the wall, results were delayed: *Had
my second scan Had my check-up Have you scheduled
your next attempt?* This roundelay they sung
when beating bounds, when they dressed urine-
      soaked hide *I had my chances*
          I saw you round/
round the corner, ivy undergrowth and marram
seed scum condensing on the pond's white eye,
the overpass above a concrete runnel feeding
back into the turbine, birds and fish: what an end –
who struggle upstream to find an outlet blocked
      Oil choked sump
        Swallowed fold
turbine blades, apertures, *Here are further scraps,
      some more of what was destroyed.*
These come to me and what can I say.

*Mucad Ibrahim, Ali Elmadani, Khaled Mustafa,
Sayyad Milne, Hussein Al-Umari, Haji-Daoud Nabi,
Kamel Darwish, Abdelfattah Qasem*
      Names drawn up in ranks
insecure as napes of their necks bent in homage,
eyes struggling out in transport on the main floor,
eyes fixed on a spot where silence is enjoined.
The angel stoops to destroy, the second names
      might be recorded,
pressed where mesh strains a crumbling sluice –

      pressed in syllables.

Fight blowback. Heartless refoulement.
            Syllable by syllable.

IMPROMPTU: LAKEFRONT TRAIL, MARCH

*Close against the lake's wall an icy snake
articulates its scales, high dense tinkle
wraps the higher hiss of the ice-freckled air.
    Iman Leila froze to death
in a half-finished concrete shell:
                  Make that internal,
Iman Leila froze to death.*

*Repeated in the undertow this belittles,
syllables that strip the infant of her
lullaby her lall, drown in the rip current
riffling through the scales beside a concrete
balustrade that girds a high rising lake.*

*I look you out again, look at you
perched in your father's elbow crook,
    look you out where I sit wrapped
by windows and the deep clanks of heating.
    Iman Leila froze to death.
        Will you take this name in,
Iman Leila who froze to death.*

RIPPLES

The lakeshore horizon is laid upon a stark road,
      the road relaxes in a long descent. A red
warning light blinks lazily,
          this way to the entrance:
its concrete brow compels visitors to dismount,
they have no choice but climb out of their taxis,

heels over head straining to resist snapping back
about a bobbin cranking pictures from outside
      spread
against a now-near wall, yellowing panopticon
rotates as their life circuit must,
          pressed tin and flash enamel push
past onset on its roundabout, its ramps closed.
Crammed it was with scooters' progress in halts.
      Terror of voltaic pile. A planisphere.
      My glass it is almost run.
      Yes those were excellent mimics
made tracks to the capitol, preached in the open,
only to rotate below the brow of such an archive.

          Counterfeit
biting earth, zero sprawled across its floral clock,
settling to besmirch what flowers had disguised –
light has to fall; what day was getting round to,
climbing frames to waver in a paddling pool,
a mini cyclone to expose a throttled rattle, shoes
          clogged with mud.
With day breaking cover petals floated upwards.

Ripples will they hold their own as pentimenti,
      rucks a flood of data inculcates in rock.

INTERRED

Insects their southern night strike up orchestral:
Warm slate accepts, but can't retain an impress
hoodwink slept lovers left when they woke;
cincture of night that defies the noisy instant
        quick-dried, the Colosseum
                concrete mass –
spotlit in the present by a moon-struck gleam
resumes motion, takes time. Bodies bolt upright,
fight shy of resting place, surfacing unswathed:
Dear, dear Grandma, again I haven't died.

On waking I scrabble through dream deposits,
hoses judder out of valves deep in the pit, spoil
        legible trustees,
                even dreams succumb
to the reign of reason, what else can be quarried
from their palimpsest: fields loll squandered,
rock conceptacles split open and body parts
surface breaking up, gleaming crushed granite,
        pink sea-shells, inked leads
                of hammered forms.
For sombre blockage angel cake ramparts swell.
Dear, dear Grandma, again I haven't died.

Drag its slate cover flush over the well's mouth.
Gouging out the stars, recruit the frets of day,
a cinching collar studded with flat diamonds;
sponge it on black windows, press back light.
        Damselflies, butterflies
              thatch tar lakes,
far fields. – These too will be desolate, sycamore
de-winged, leaves fall, bees will fail to message
between rust-spotted wheat stalks. Wind squats
on parking spots, rubberised perimeters shrink.
Dear, dear Grandma, again I haven't died.

CONCRETE

Can the same forest answer to the range of stone,
crew of that stone skiff cinching the horizon?
Stone men steer their boat incandescent round a
channel between day and full density of night
         Shadow now concrete
                 Dirt swept aside.
The grey carrier farther out is detaining birds
within its ropes, Ark Royal but no hawk lifts off,
no creature disembarks. A dock of stone snaps
to attention at its gunwales, camouflaging vents
        on managed waste,
             fistula I think
rips in the air plugged with birdsong. Concrete
is billowing, a fragile tent, a stencilled hide
shook out from the tannery. A caulker's hammer
times blows, thunder sheet seams are soldered,
       languorous felt
           braced against canvas
tacked up to suppress noise, the native insects
shrink to one frequency, hearing concentrates
inside its hood of elegantly stitched deerskin.
Collect then in the same forest's auditory zone
        swarms that hang
           muffling his ears,
and from the outer ring, the skiff impassive men
pilot between death and life, a paralysis steals,
bees stagger on the hum he's listening-in to,
his own hum now pervades his bee-dead hood.

STRAND

Detached they whiten as on waves a cork float does,
boulders crusted with their work to stay put.
These had not mapped
their course, but phosphorescent in entrainment
        achieve some perch, some poise

Beach.

What else was there for it? Dawns must double, icy
moons above a parapet
someone keeps an eye peeled for, multiply. What the
host gets up to looks violent and conformist,
        answering a call

scarcely audible, not so much the ocean's mutability
as undertow of drowned forebears
shaping every word now uttered, hauling back
like base shingle, above whom the unmoored toss
nevertheless resonant

Ditch.

Pink spirals of the turban shells are winkled out and
flattened writhe naked in a living mat up to a sea
again and again falling flat.
The earlier re-masses, collapsing itself.
Void chambers strew the beach, anechoic.
        What scores the horizon

Ketch.
A long vaulted passage winding through a sandbank.

IMPROMPTU: LAKE OF NEMI

How doth the city sit solitary!,
    the lake shore lies desolate.
Unyielding is the sessile oak,
bee-busy, the eroding wall yet stares;
arms of ivy interfold on its face,
countermanding, muscling back.

Edict took its stark form,
a wall against these shape-shifters,
    rabble without passports,
slaves, the transported,
subject to no heading, to no name.
    Don't be disturbed, wanderer,

carried on your swollen music,
garlanded where you go:
    if with dynt the rynde is riven,
face pitted and jounced,
    if detached heads poke
through glossy leaves,
offensive with their stench of decay:

The ivy barrier swarms yet,
a queen drinks in her tribute.

ROOD

The wood meets the wound in its revolving circle.
A point has been inferred from the circumference,
      point tentative as these:
rubber hits the road because it mortifies in spikes,

too-fragile seams grace day; scratched at by birds,
sky retreats to lemon sherbet, blood
corruption has been graded down from indigo
according to a test stick,
only the deflated resting awkwardly on their rims
      relish agony –
having come to the point, lowering onto the rock.

This declivity, this shallow saucer shrugs.
Stand on your shadow as a shadow goes concrete.
Windows opposite at twilight bring furnishings
face-forward, faces there press
against the day's sash hauled up as the sun drops

unchecked by particles, by their festoons.
Where is the wound the blank unimpressionable
      long to pass through,
the cracks in the rood screen, the suffering forest?

Interiors get mounted, they yearn for their thorns.

AMBASSADOR

Reflected belt of stars in the centre of a moulding
encasing a watered ellipse –
                                  mahogany
cartouche for a cheval-glass, flecked, foxed
with atropine, appraisals and moues: cover that,
      use the satin square.

Blink in the oval to smithereens a pitted watchful
look, purging it pixel by pixel:
      a tongue-depressor, clutter on a nightstand,
creamy neutral plaster, purge all until a void
distinguished only by a single nail from which
might once have hung or be intended yet to hang

key sigils for a portrait, set of teeth, pair of eyes,
a wound, a heart, an arrow –
until a void shimmers as above the risen lake.
                Flip the glass whose moulding
will be breached, the warp and skew of grimaces
      slops down, returning underwater.

When will a nail blossom? When swells the ovoid?
What drapes from the thorn is a baby's lorn cry.
What sags from a pilaster hook is a stretch skull.

STORE

Flower-heads lean as though attentive, and beasts
listen not for weakness but a startle of their kind,

so blackened skin that's hung like seaweed across
a chair's back, twitches to resume its shape in light,

for all the chair's naked ribs set little store by it
but merely support as does a banner whose device

tempts oblivion, dips its once flaunted sigil.
                                                           Scalene
a ladder-back looms over malls of human motive,

terraces where coats were thrown aside, gloves
strewn across a marble face, where water features

leaving residue in sand under tiled news displays,
crawl reflectionless below to enter their updates.

A silhouette is flaking off a roadhouse tympanum,
its sleek original steps into night. Twilight birds –

they strip fat away so in wind ribs moan and sigh.

CRUISE

Below decks SUVs shift uneasily where strapped down
seeping oil, awash with holy oil. There had been rafts
barred from coastal waters, daily news,
        coastguards, fast navy vessels
buzzing them with violent wash.
        Keep them down, in waiting facilities.
        Sweat them amidst shackled cars, in kitchens,
        deeper to plug the bilges.
Do not deviate from course. Then the turbines sputter.

Becalmed on global voyager, gold and platinum decks,
refused at every quayside practiced in refusal, people
of high profile, indignant and resourceful;
        no washing hands of such people,
once land subdues securely underfoot for them,
        where surely land should be set.
Who boarded the world with their tax-free,
        washed audit trail,
        their wake of scrubbed shit,
time poisons in their citadel, insinuates bars and salons;

stone crew servants in their epaulettes and crisp whites
sicken, ball courts have been shut down,
life and death trials rigged as always but evidently.
        Go down below decks
        between skeletal ribs.
The citadel transported on a dayworker raft,
        raft conveyed on a dying sea,
        oceans wrapped about a fateful,
hard rubber ball that ricochets about the heavenly court,

ellipse it pings off at odd angles, murders the incautious
drinking mojitos, chattering and betting on survival.
I found a job working in the fields,
picking apples, peaches, cherries, asparagus, squash,
and cucumber. I went hungry.
My name is Guadalupe Navarro Hernandez.
        No resource is stuffed in this name.
Build him a boat, pitch the sky's superstructure
as the boat on its stone raft overlays ocean. Now
change everything, warm the oil for libations. Now sail.

BEACHED

Could those heart's strings be those slackening
        visibly in the inspection slot,
            ten wire strings
strum tinnily, cousin to a kind of native abacus,
beads long-lost,
            slack strings ping and twang:
        How can the pegs be wiggled free?
when so stiff they seem bonded to their pegbox.

Time having passed, they'll slip, lose their grip,
        drumhead levers open,
          supple reeds split apart.
Intent performers
throb rhythm out in sea, sand and sonic ribbing,
scalloping the shore,
        but pulling back under pressure,
twisting tightly crack. The reaches are indefinite,

markless, drear; sandflies jerk and leave no trace
on a blank sheet under a blank sky
leaving no impress either.
            Count your blessings,
rolling down the frictionless
length up to the breakwater, listen out
        for those sandflies that infest
derelict sound holes, *anyone who ever had a heart*.

CRYSTAL

Labour of the empty hive had been left to rot
                crystallised and winking.
Below a mica sheet dead bees lie piled.
            Turbulent heat.
On this hot day an engineer crouches
naked before the hive –
            a robe of worker bees, a moving fleece
swagging off his shoulders,
his voice above the cushion of their humming
            lifted in descant.
                  It was the anthology
of sweet flowers made his strings lose tension.
It was their concentrate, their distillate.
            Poisonous chords.
            Severally.
Unconsoling light glancing off his sheaf of wires.
So now he would strike savagely, their sound
            submissive to his hand.

Breathing will accord with insects' sonic pulse:
theirs is the ardour,
ardour in his violence would shock earth to form
            a lump of crystal, self-tuned,
gleaming in its confidence, its charm,
knowing not one drop of its medium.
            Breathing draws its fill of the loaded
floral periods.
Breaks capsules of the world's wonders,
            so reduced.
                  Mechanisms fall apart.
                  Strings had slackened.
            Nothing doing
held further counsel and still does. One note
shivers, every splinter interposes the one note,
burying the idiom of song under clips
            poisonous to bees.
            Resonance becomes the rule of plasma,
and of its children icy and gaseous.

IMPROMPTU: THE DECAPITATED OAK

In clarity, in exactitude before the light, but not light alone, its flickering field –
against merger and indistinction –
against loss of the possibility of merger –
    the rind that matters –
    that slops can be constrained to a perfect point –
    no danger of affection or response –
only the property to self-present as is –
    the rind, the edge –
not the object within but the object that makes of itself a gift through a fissure.

GLINTING

To be seduced by pools of scent,
        drawn up as if a clock on a rose mount,
entreated by stars lost against dawn, to arise.
              Birds tempt for it is spring,
their solemn cantilever weighs little
next to the entreaty of the stars withdrawing.

Blinders to blinding on the hill flank, scribble
        hurried takes, scrawl
across the openings clouds soon unmask.
          Jarring frames
drop on the awoken waiting at day's border.

Shape them, though long since their engineers
        rattled shutters over holts,
resilient they must push back,
              dislocating dawn for what is;
love shielded with elaborate shifting emotions,

implicit under evidence. Will stars reappear?
     Matt stone winks.
Not a wink of sunlight when refracted, tremor
            off intelligent quartz –
the fields too pop and prickle. Granite folds.
Clay cracks. Earth shapes up. Birds build.

HARROW

Were they not conscripts, conscripts first in each
other's eyes,
       rise calligraphic from their
              black, crow-mandated
slate underneath
which the wedges splitting white into cuneiform
shards the climb's desirous fat advancing
what it cannot have or do, deposits not-having
symbionts glistened off lipid gems, that molten
       long filtered drop by drop –

between such items can an outflow deflect round
a silhouette departing lovers will have left press
of over air? – softly solicitous –
       Scratch of a swan's quill, court hand,
jerks up to a line whose insistence drawing forth
       something out of nothing,

blindsided skin feather-stroked once electrostatic
       lengthy moan such longing howl,
oh oh cursive is stretching out.
How thin air is yet it clings in its opaque
droplets in a cloud chamber,
                   secretive it is still.
       Dreams thicken,
no, decentralise: feeders but whose interchange
closes any ramp for dispersal,
       conscripted to be that single cluster
imposing nothing,
codicil outweighing any provision of the will.

CALAIS

Among the facing armies all can see the likeness,
brought to a halt disconcerted. Clouds, distant
hills become authorities they consent to live by,
even the same plate of food served repeatedly:
     Them and us.

Against one white cheek the settled world rests.
It presently amassed until now European White
weighs upon each once thought free weightless.
Knowing what was to know one slides towards:

    Will you listen to us now
our lips are sewn, will you see us now
we stand blind in front of you? Bereft of our names.

Blue sky their mantle of plastic sheeting, cloud
all the food will cross their lips, cameras track
silhouettes against a shadow flank, recognising
faces thrown between sectors. Face of the police
     sewn upon a like face –

I thought in your arms I would be free
but blue skies direct their legs with hankering,
hills are pressing down, holding each to blame
for their fate: how could it be more in their face:
blind fate is the meal we present to our likeness.

AGNI

We thrive in the day before the day but circulate
more slowly under the dissolving shelves, songs
reverse-engineer into the poison germ of seeds
packed in the crop and unfledge into a potage, for

this is the set-aside, the off-shoring out of mind,
*Asifa Bano's small lifeless body, eight years old,
raped repeatedly in the temple precincts*, out of sight.
And the fire is discernible only at the perimeter,

fringing each object prone to our use, consuming
fire invisible to worshippers of things, *our* things
contracting out, shrunk into perfect marvels
staggeringly heavy when fire and deaths are taken

back into the thing's shrunken compass. Living
as we do in the day we commit to function, put out
the empties, recycle through the day after next,
shelves dissolve, the Heraclitan fire licks the edge

of the black, dead, high-definition screen, shrunk
down to a watch dial, shrunk *so he could rape her
one final time*. Revenge that zone-encircled waist
burns our chaff and cremates all songs melodious.

IMPROMPTU: FOR THE FALLEN

My own hostage, surely I should free my heart
to fall back in spray and in heather, that expansiveness:
*   This is asphalt and I rebuff the invitation.*
What can beauty instigate if the base of a delta,
*   cut-away,*
laps against immeasurable horizons, beauty but
a dream of no borders, where all things
can arrive through home delivery. They take it on them,
those claiming the front,
*   their neglect or disappointment, push*
the pushed-down back behind linking arms,
*   march for the ineloquent,*
embarrassing, the unphotogenic, always spoken-for,
*   give yourself that:*
but does dilation into sunrise not disdain the street,
concrete kerb,
*   the falling-back leave cold*
drowned bodies on the downside of its heather, mauve
of its tidal ripple, creased sand.
*   Must beauty*
gloss, must it glimmer, must it inveigle: shall beauty
*   roar. Barry MacSweeney says yes.*
*   Gwendolyn Brooks says yes, Sean Bonney.*
I am too well-spoken, hostage to this voice box –: conch,
now call me out.

THISTLEDOWN

Husks corresponding thin out as mere interface,
in sequence, whale pods uprise for a TV spot,
fawns dapple in a slalom of indivisible fences,
these promise the desired clench of synchrony:
        each as it were
                of its own right
tore at filaments, tore restraints,
pegged out in drying hides behind fenced trees.
Distant bells, massed people's choirs: a sentinel
calls from a caulked roof, time's weapon blunts,
no seal shall smear or melt, everything aligns
        to one fringed disc, arrow
            stilled by night,
hyphen hovering by day
links hemispheres, instructs them in a vacuum,
leaves continents or dustheaps ridged along the
outer banks, in their succession of chalkmarks.
        None had loved enough what
they must find by losing. The days worn ragged
show mastic where rubbed thin

as what's lost parades in forms aching for ful-
filment overwhelming what each to each tallies.
        Mistake to make love, O
imperfect, marked oddments; peck a flowering
thistle for a soft swathed seed might be enough.

POND-LIFE

      Proximity as such as a formal mode of
fucking, mud-packs thickening desire to cement,
      each sidles into life
            life off-centre
puncturing the tympanum,
flames that lick fairly around their functional rim:

living humans snap to it, head to tail as function,
lambent out of the corner of an eye, a suspect
twists in mid-air seeking to detach, style rankings
      slide across the board,
           all time in joint

rejigs to the frequency a bodyguard's earpiece sets.
      Thick bass notes dissolve,
earth falls away and a stream of plasma bubbles
winks in an endless soap opera.
                Switch off, go off-grid,

yet streaming will persist,
      controlled by the atomic clock
           off-ramp. Out of sheer want, go with it.
Thicken with sediment that substitutes for touch.

FRONTIER

A satyr's pelt twitches where it's thrilling still to
its alternating voice, back and forth is bit-perfected,
combing out contrary protocols, assayed fleas,
finding ecstasy in disembodied senses and their
capture by their own ceaseless erethism. Smells
wealthy, like a leather settle in a prepped loft,
sounds authentic, swells like the song of the earth;
that apportions, drops spiralling like apple peel,
sliced horizon floating in polypropylene packs:
do these revert too, things not being as they were,
that never as they were, were, horizoned by their
lost horizons, circumscribed by their lost frontier?
      World of toys
               Lifestyle cockroaches
sealed in freezer bags, to appearances stay active –
canoes go nosing though distilled water threads,
oarsmen pose in ceremonial attire, glue ears
cocked for birdsong, promising to GPS the studio
where purity is mocked up, virtues renovated.
Culture warriors buddy round a pristine font
supped as if burbling springs and stocked rivers
focused at a single jet playing just within hearing,
one voice assured of its audition on a plush floor:
I feel like there's something alive in my body and I
      don't know what it is.

STOP-OUT

Every replicant gets tanned like a purse or wallet,
count them out, they are at a loss awful to bear,
work of a deep manufactory of joints, eyes, lights
still in pre-production, you can be my best self,
mindful of the company that came together, hip
lassitude shrugs to a perfect fit, take five it's toady
style. Why, that had been our own tune way back,
when the circle stayed unbroken, generative boss
shone with the name bestowed by our language,
that no perspective would budge. Filch from it
bucketloads of jetsam sequenced then encrusted,
charred like a transom beam fire is finished with
   Salt, weed and barnacles
   Fistful of pills
their mental discipline, did they populate a gloss
pornography of the threatened, water writhing
in its confines at lakeside, racing for the shore,
spilt across paths, surface blazing toxin-bright
with Asian carp and other invasive species? This
cannot fit, must not. An antique turquoise bead
breaks on a circlet. A pod of seals breaks as the
waves compete with each other for the shoreline,
hills mount to a prospect. We own it all deniably.
What has been filled in permits no flow, squeegee
   pulls down the screen,
     fistfuls of weed.

POLYVERSE

      Shake the tambourine, throw the bones,
humans and other chattels daisy-chain in motion,
slamming hard against each other
              whenever cars brake:
deer pelts are spread out to be sewn, the repeater
heard across the tracked but unscarred terrain,
lightly-ridden smashed by the pick and share:

      hear the hum, hear the whistle spirits
vent in their cyclical self-test, telling each it owns

effectively the full available frequency range,
Louisiana Purchase, the Alaska, the New Mexico,
                  singing of the open
road while wrested into fur comforts,
             trimming
ragged pelts, leaving stragglers on the arid waste
          beyond the culverts tidy and managed:

hydraulic economy where water finds its idiom,
      priced back through a grating to a
sweet source whose rights were bought:

                    nomads who had waited on
their star by night's well, their turn for water, dip
buckets at a signal, shuffle forward:
              fugue of the parched
heard through juddering sewer pipes and qanats,

interweaves as blowback swells to meet due time,
puts pressure on the cistern to release full flow.

IMPROMPTU: IN THE TORCH-LIT WOOD

A lowlife, a loser
moving like a breath across the muddled lake,
   stirring weeds,
rucks the film of water, and it might seem
   prints the hurrying matrices
with bar-codes, written on water;
and failing hands are seen to revolve below
from above,
and above from below,
   paying out the lead from the prow,
waxed so what adheres is any jettisoned shell
from the now-extraneous world.
   In troublous times
by dint of shallow armature,
broken forms will dissipate. The sun itself
   commanded to appear,
sees its face so broken it retreats
behind the wood circle,
   a deity's force
dissolves in a grid of light too much like gold,
and nothing like.

UPLOAD

What fire can pierce the frozen lake, will it be sun
whose summer's memory was stopped in opacity –
      but hoisted in spring the sun trickles
down on no negative; black will cast a blue shade,
call it heaven for a moment, treetops feather
a wood circle, denied to reflection so tending blue:
in that quarter the wind lies, eyes follow needily.

Does a fixed plunge, the plummet put in its show?
The wanderer as would be is compelled by a blade
whirring overhead, directionless, such hesitancy.
      A mighty handle fixed to a dead plank.
A faded photograph sunk into bark.
Is this the brazier where children were sacrificed;
      when will this scattershot, this arrow
find its mark in him, scar this inadvertent voyeur?

A glacial erratic, blue iris floats above the humour
churning beneath. What would be lucid muddies,
what would be turbid, bakes; the answering deep
of hot magma, echo of the solar supremacy,
supports a spitting eye children are flung onto,
      that cannot see its own depths.
      Ghosts flee but lack agility
enough to revive; votaries adore their murderer,
before dying from a train of plagues and defences.

Barefoot on the ice sways the hurdy-gurdy man;
a bow that had drawn a living note turns a wheel
scratching slack strings. The shadow he projects
climbs like an eclipse pinned between sun and pit,
      he has been transfixed
by a nocturnal beauty while the buried sun spills
heat down the highways and burns from below.

© 2021 by John Wilkinson

Published by The Last Books
Amsterdam, the Netherlands, and Sofia, Bulgaria

www.thelastbooks.org

Designed and typeset by Phil Baber
Cover artwork by Elisabeth Rafstedt
Printed and bound by Wilco

ISBN 978-9-49178-015-8

Much gratitude is owed for support
to the Division of the Humanities,
University of Chicago.